I0047075

© Copyright 2018 Kaye Publicity, Inc.

All rights reserved.

You are only permitted to use the content as expressly authorized by Kaye Publicity, Inc., or the specific content provider. Except for a single copy made for personal use only, you may not copy, reproduce, modify, republish, upload, post, transmit, or distribute any content or information from this workbook in any form or by any means without prior written permission from Kaye Publicity, Inc., or the specific content provider, and you are solely responsible for obtaining permission before reusing any copyrighted material that is available within.

Any unauthorized use of the materials referred to may violate copyright, trademark and other applicable laws and could result in criminal or civil penalties.

"Your brand is what other people say about you when you're not in the room."

— *Jeff Bezos, founder of Amazon.com*

Introduction

When most people think of a "brand" they think of consumer products like Kellogg's or Lexus. But whether you're branding a person or a breakfast cereal, the purpose is the same:

1. To convey a clear message in a short amount of time
2. To establish name recognition and make you memorable

Think of a product like Starbucks. As soon as you hear the name or see that green and while mermaid, you immediately think of the Seattle-based coffee chain. You think of your favorite drink, the unique sizes, maybe even the music they play over the loudspeaker. You can taste the pumpkin spice. You know that no matter which location you go to, the drinks, service, and ambiance will be the same. It's a known entity.

A brand conveys who you are, what you do, and what makes you unique in a succinct way. This workbook, paired with the Personal Brand Master Class, will guide you through the process of creating a memorable and favorable personal brand. This may take time, and your tagline and brand message may change over time. Refer back to this workbook frequently, and don't be afraid to adjust or start fresh as you add new services and products. While a brand should be consistent, it doesn't have to be set in stone.

As always, if you need guidance or additional resources, don't hesitate to connect at BrandingOutsidetheBox.com or in the Facebook group!

Notes/Ideas/Inspiration

"Too many companies want their brands to reflect some idealized, perfected image of themselves. As a consequence, their brands acquire no texture, no character and no public trust."

— *Richard Branson*

Identify

Your personal brand is made up of a simple equation: **Who you are + What you do + What makes you unique = Your personal brand**.

But identifying the correct values to that equation proves a bit more complex. Use this branding worksheet to identify your true brand elements and then craft your brand messaging.

Notes/Ideas/Inspiration

Who are you?

What do you do?

What sets you apart from others in the field?

Identify

What are you passionate about?

What is your worldview?

What is your philosophy?

How do you want people to see you?

What do you hope to do in the next 5 years?

Tagline & Brand Summary

Use this section to create a 1-2 line elevator pitch or tagline. This is what you'll use when introducing yourself to people at networking events, on the homepage of your website, and as your short bio on your social media pages.

Use this section to create a 1-2 paragraph brand summary which serves as a longer explanation of your personal brand. It can be used to answer follow up questions after you deliver your tagline, on the About page of your website, or as the longer bio on your social media platforms.

Your brand summary should convey a feeling or idea of who you are and what you're about. When you think of Lexus, you don't automatically think of all the various makes, models and colors they sell. When you think Lexus, you think luxury. You associate Gatorade with hydration and athletic performance. What do people associate with you?

Full Mission Statement

Nearly all companies and organizations have mission statements, so you should too! This expands on your brand summary to include your long term goals, your brand values, and other insight into what makes you unique. You may be the only one to ever see this mission statement, but it will inform all your decision-making going forward.

Notes/Ideas/Inspiration

"Personal branding is about managing your name—even if you don't own a business—in a world of misinformation, disinformation, and semi-permanent Google records. Going on a date? Chances are that your 'blind' date has Googled your name. Going to a job interview? Ditto."

— Tim Ferriss

Establish

Once you've identified your personal brand, the next step is to establish that brand online. The end goal is to ensure that everyone in your life, from your Twitter followers to your boss, has a clear understanding of your brand, and as a result, remembers you and thinks of you favorably.

Take the following steps to ensure that your online footprint conveys your brand message and reaches your target audience.

Google Yourself. What are the top 5 results?

1.

2.

3.

4.

5.

Click on each of these results. Do they convey your personal brand message? Are these results you want people to see?

If yes, then great! Move on to the next step! If no, here are some actions you can take to replace some of those less-than-desirable search results:

- **Contribute a guest blog or article to a high-traffic website**
- **Increase activity on one or more of your social platforms**
- **Update your current website with fresh content**
- **Put links to your website on every social platform you own**

Establish

Notes/Ideas/Inspiration

Think about your target audience (customers, clients, potential employers, etc.). Where do they get their information?

What social media platforms do they utilize?

➦ Action: Create an active presence on these platforms.

Where do they get their news?

➦ Action: Pitch yourself for an interview or contribute a guest article to these outlets.

Do they prefer reading, viewing, or listening to content?

➦ Action: Create content using their preferred medium.

After taking these actions, wait a few weeks, then google yourself again. Are you more satisfied with the results?

"I've learned that people will forget what you said, people will forget what you did, but people will never forget how you made them feel."

— *Maya Angelou*

Content Strategy

Now that you understand how to establish your online platform, it's time to figure out what you're going to say. The content you share online, whether it's your website copy, tweets, or Instagram photos, should be authentic and a part of who you are (emphasis on part.)

To develop your content strategy, we start with a brainstorm:

Where do you live?

Who's in your family?

What do you do in your spare time?

What causes are you passionate about?

What else makes you YOU?

Notes/Ideas/Inspiration

Content Strategy

Go through your responses and jot down what each of these characteristics say about you. For example, the fact that you're a vegetarian and only buy organic may say that you're concerned about animals, the environment, and what goes into your body. If you live in New York City, it says that you're an urbanite and that you're used to fast-moving environments.

Now that you see what message each of your characteristics convey, highlight the ones you want to keep in your content strategy. If you work for an environmental protection agency or represent an organic food company, then your vegetarianism would be a welcome addition to your personal brand. But if you're working in finance, it won't do anything to enhance your brand message.

Decide which topics will be included in your content strategy and list them here:

Content Strategy

Every time you consider posting to social media, writing a blog post, or participating in an interview, refer back to the list. You may be tempted to re-tweet something about the election, post the cutest photo of your kid to Facebook, or Instagram pictures of your food, but if it's not a part of your content strategy, then don't. When you're at a work function or other networking event, people may ask you about your family or your hobbies, and while you shouldn't lie, you shouldn't focus on them either. Steer conversations towards your brand topics, or redirect the conversation back to the other person. If you're asked to do a radio interview or speak at a conference, scrutinize the topic and platform. Does it fall in line with your content strategy?

No? Then politely decline.

Notes/Ideas/Inspiration

Platform

Your platform is more than a website, media appearances, or your speaking career. Those things help establish your brand and expand your name recognition, but your platform is actually about your audience and their ability to take action.

Audience is a key ingredient in establishing your platform, and that audience can take many forms.

Where is your audience? Check all that apply and include number of followers/subscribers:

- ☐ Mailing list ____
- ☐ Blog subscribers ____
- ☐ Twitter ____
- ☐ Facebook page____
- ☐ Facebook group ____
- ☐ Instagram ____
- ☐ Youtube ____
- ☐ Pinterest ____
- ☐ Group program or mastermind ____
- ☐ Club or team that meets in person ____
- ☐ Others (list below)

Notes/Ideas/Inspiration

Platform

Social media followers alone don't equal a platform. Neither does a lucrative speaking career or high profile media appearances. What's important is how you integrate all these components to create an *engaged audience* that will take action on your behalf.

After people are introduced to your work, do they sign up for your mailing list? Do they come out to a meet-up? Do you parlay that media appearance into a regular contributor position? What can you do to engage your new audience and establish a platform? How can you keep the conversation going with your clients, your readers, your audience?

Here are some examples of what the process of converting viewers or new contacts to loyal, rabid fans looks like:

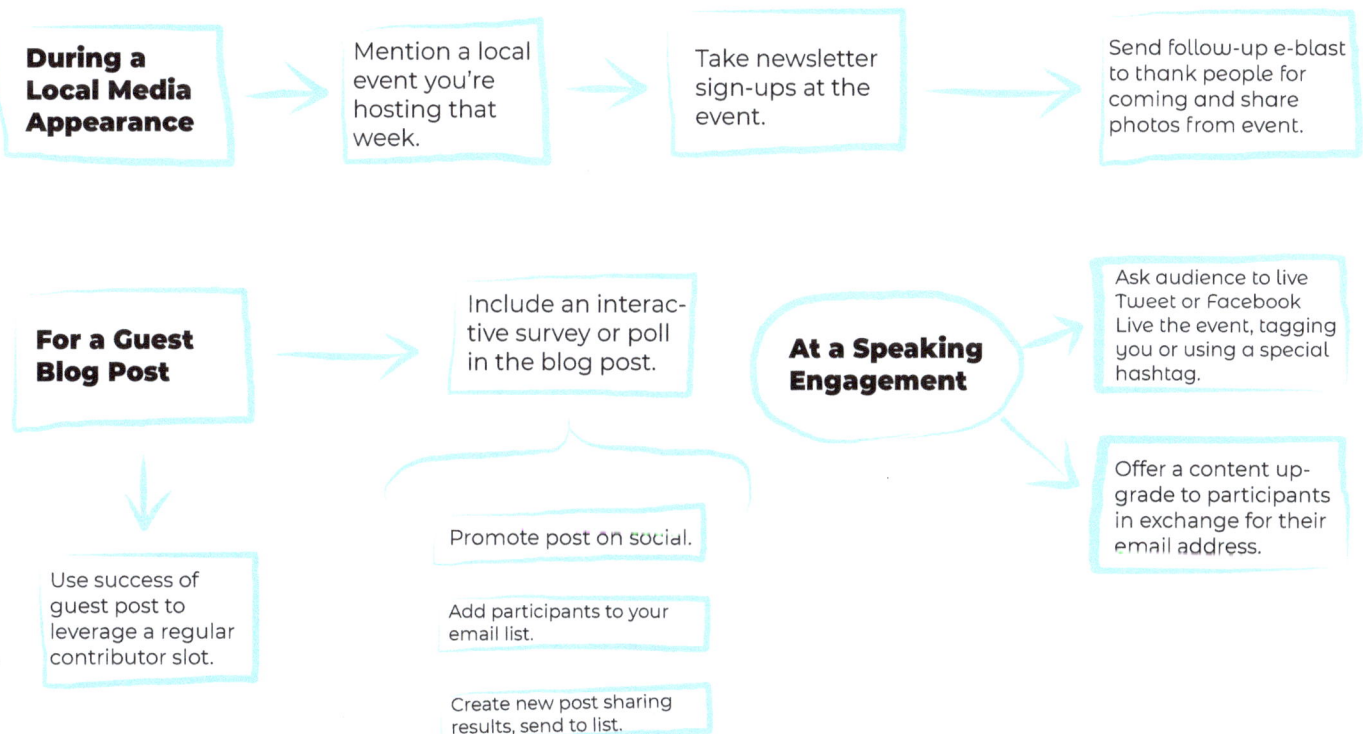

During a Local Media Appearance → Mention a local event you're hosting that week. → Take newsletter sign-ups at the event. → Send follow-up e-blast to thank people for coming and share photos from event.

For a Guest Blog Post → Include an interactive survey or poll in the blog post. → Promote post on social. / Add participants to your email list. / Create new post sharing results, send to list.

Use success of guest post to leverage a regular contributor slot.

At a Speaking Engagement → Ask audience to live Tweet or Facebook Live the event, tagging you or using a special hashtag. → Offer a content upgrade to participants in exchange for their email address.

How can you convert your audience into a platform? On the next page, brainstorm as many process ideas like the flowcharts above as you can.

Platform

Brainstorm Your Ideas Here.

"Style is a simple way of saying complicated things."

— Jean Cocteau

Appearance

Clothes don't just make the man, they make the brand. Your appearance conveys more of your brand as you realize and serves as your first opportunity to create brand recognition. Before you introduce yourself, deliver your elevator pitch, even tweet, your audience will look at your exterior. It's crucial this exterior conveys your brand message.

Some of your appearance will be determined by your industry; if you're working at a law or accounting firm, you can't wear jeans and t-shirts just because they're on-brand. And depending on where you're going and whom you're meeting with, you may have to adjust your look. But there should be consistent themes in your appearance, which keep your brand message consistent. Consider the following:

Red: Powerful, not afraid to stand out or make a statement

Orange: Energetic, unique, not afraid to stand out

Yellow: Happy, fun, positive, and more feminine

Green: Comforting and easy going

Blue: Loyal, confident, successful, also calm

Purple: The color of royalty, luxury, sophisticated

Pink: Comforting, compassionate, and feminine

Black: A leader, powerful, classic

White: Innocent, pure, and optimistic

Brown: Grounded, earthy, well-balanced

Gray: Subtle, blends in, doesn't want to draw attention

Appearance

Style

Notes/Ideas/Inspiration

For many of you who work in corporate, it may seem difficult to branch out and establish a personal style. The key is working within the confines of the industry to make style choices that convey your message. Are you...

High fashion – You're ahead of current fashion trends (which sometimes means standing out), you don't mind spending a little extra to have something that's one of a kind.

Classic – You opt for plain clothes, classic tailoring, and timeless style. The only statement you want to make with your clothes is "professional."

Vintage – You can often be found wearing vintage costume jewelry, a 50's dress, or a suit/vest/suspender combo.

Eccentric – You don't shy away from patterns and funky accessories. You want to have fun with your wardrobe.

Signature Pieces

A signature article of clothing or accessory can trigger a person's memory and help you make a more lasting impression. Think of Steve Jobs's black turtleneck or Mark Zuckerberg's grey t-shirt and jeans. When you think of them, you can immediately picture them.

Appearance

You don't have to commit to wearing the same thing every day (though it does help cut down on shopping time!). Instead, opt for a signature accessory, such as...

Notes/Ideas/Inspiration

☆ **Funky, colorful socks**

☆ **Bowtie**

☆ **Suspenders**

☆ **Vest under the suit**

☆ **Necklace, bracelet, or watch**

You can also use a signature print like always wearing floral or plaid. Whatever you choose, it should help convey your brand message while staying within industry norms.

Use this space to write down your "Branded Appearance." What will people always see you wearing and what does it say about you?

"An ugly personality destroys a pretty face."

— *unknown*

Public Persona

Though your appearance will serve as your first impression, what you say when you open your mouth will serve as your second. As we addressed in the Content Strategy section, what you say plays an integral role in your personal brand, but how you say it is just as important.

When people hear the word "persona" they often think of something fake, but really, a persona is actually a portion of your authentic self.

Fill out the following:

Which characteristics describe your personality?

☐ **Opinionated**　　　☐ **Straightforward**

☐ **Easy-going**　　　☐ **Soft-spoken**

☐ **Task-driven**　　　☐ **Blunt**

☐ **Shy**　　　☐ **Dreamer**

☐ **Reserved**　　　☐ **Pragmatic**

☐ **Happy**　　　☐ **Confident**

☐ **Cynical**　　　☐ **Creative**

☐ **Positive**　　　☐ **Outgoing**

☐ **Skeptical**　　　☐ **Big-picture focused**

☐ **Driven**　　　☐ **Forward thinking**

Are you a/an... (circle one)

Introvert	Extrovert
Optimist	Pessimist

Notes/Ideas/Inspiration

Public Persona

Are you a... (circle one)

Doer	Manager	Creator

Do you:
- [ ] Make decisions based on research and logic
- [ ] Go with your gut

Do you:
- [ ] Plan everything
- [ ] Go with the flow

Do you:
- [ ] Look forward to and predict future trends
- [ ] Focus on what's happening now

Of these key elements, which ones contribute to your brand?

Notes/Ideas/Inspiration

The next time you go to a meeting, deliver a speech, or host a Facebook Live post, make sure that only those characteristics show!

"Even when you are marketing to your entire audience or customer base, you are still simply speaking to a single human at any given time."

— Ann Handley

Engagement

Building a personal brand is like maintaining a garden: It requires ongoing care, the needs will change depending on the environment, and, if left unattended, it will perish. You can't just create a tagline, give yourself a makeover, grow an audience, then sit back and relax. You must continue to build your platform, establish your public persona, and expand your name recognition. You must continue to engage.

How will you let your audience know that you're paying attention to them? (Examples: Surveys and polls, online Q&As, one-on-one meetings)

Why should someone continue to follow you? What value are you delivering? How are you serving your audience?

Notes/Ideas/Inspiration

"A goal without a plan is just a wish."

— Antoine de Saint-Exupéry

Your Personal Brand Plan

Now that you understand the seven steps to launching your personal brand, it's time to map out your Personal Brand Plan. Creating a successful brand does not happen overnight and it requires ongoing effort.

The first step is to know where you're going. Imagine yourself, your life, your business or career in six months. Take a few moments to write down what that looks like for you. What kinds of work are you doing? How much are you making? What does your day-to-day life look like?

Based on what you've already worked through in this process, what are three things you could do to help you achieve those goals? Maybe it's something simple like building your brand/persona wardrobe. Maybe it's booking a special event or getting a gig you've been after. Or perhaps you've got a platform or networking goal to reach out to a certain number of followers or build your email list to a specific number. Write down your three goals.

On the next page, you'll create your six-month Personal Brand Plan to achieve those three goals.

Six Month Personal Brand Plan

Month					
What tactics will you use to establish your brand?					
What content will you create?					
How will you engage your audience?					
Other opportunities to convey your personal brand? (Speaking gigs, networking events, etc.)					

"When you have a strong personal brand, you don't chase after promotions, clients, and customers...

people chase after you."

— Dana Kaye

About the author

Dana Kaye is a veteran publicist, social media pro, and brand manager. In 2009, she founded Kaye Publicity, Inc., a boutique PR company specializing in publishing and entertainment. Known for her innovative ideas and knowledge of current trends, she coaches her clients on how to identify and establish their unique personal brands. Kaye is also the author of *Your Book, Your Brand: The Step-by-Step Guide to Launching Your Book and Boosting Your Sales*, and the creator of Branding Outside the Box, where she helps driven entrepreneurs and aspiring leaders become more memorable and make more meaningful connections.

Connect with Dana at

BrandingOutsidetheBox.com

Facebook.com/danakaye23

Instagram.com/danakaye23

Twitter.com/dana_kaye

Youtube.com/c/danakaye23

www.ingramcontent.com/pod-product-compliance
Lightning Source LLC
Chambersburg PA
CBHW050241220326
41598CB00047B/7474